Banana

Creatures

Make Your Own

Iryna Stepanova

Sergiy Kabachenko

FIREFLY BOOKS

Contents

Introduction 3
Man 4
Ram 6
Rooster 8
Snail 10
Poodle 12
Dragon 14
Bull 16
Grizzly Bear 18
Rabbit 20
Cat 22
Fly 24
Lion...................................... 26
Seahorse.............................. 28
Scorpion 30
Tiger..................................... 32
Mouse................................... 34
Gnome 36
Pirate 39
Face 42
Mermaid................................ 44
Pig 46
Prowling Lion........................ 48

Hedgehog 50
Frog...................................... 52
Turtle 54
Butterfly 56
Centipede.............................. 58
Young Guy 60
Crocodile............................... 62
Crab 64
Horse 66
Flowers.................................. 68
Dog 70
Ostrich 72
Clown 75
Giraffe 78
Monkey 80
Parrot.................................... 82
Bird....................................... 84
Flower 86
Palm Tree and Monkey 88
Aster 90
Rat 92
Octopus 94

Introduction

Bananas have been called the "paradise fruit" because this delicacy comes to us from the "heavenly places" in Southeast Asia. Many people in this region still believe that the serpent tempted Adam and Eve with a banana.

There are more than 40 kinds of bananas, but today we mainly eat only a few specially cultivated species. The banana tree is considered one of the tallest species of herbs, with a height of up to 30 feet (9 meters). The fruits grow in tassels and may include anywhere from several tens to hundreds of bananas in each bunch.

The banana is also one of the oldest cultivated plants in the world. The first mention of the banana was found in Buddhist writings dating back to around 500 BCE. Later, descriptions of this fruit were found in the works of ancient philosophers in India, China, Greece and Rome.

The raw banana contains 89 calories per 100 g of product. It is non-greasy and highly nutritious, thanks to its high carbohydrate count, as well as high fiber and valuable vitamin and mineral content. The latter includes vitamins A, B1, B2, B3, B6, B12, C, E; and macro- and microelements such as calcium, potassium, sodium, magnesium, niacin, folic acid, phosphorus, copper, iron and zinc. Of particular importance is the banana's content of the amino acid tryptophan, from which our body produces serotonin (the "happiness hormone"). Eating one or two bananas can have a positive impact on your mood.

We often consume bananas as a dessert and use in their raw form for the preparation of cakes, pastries, chocolates, ice cream, jellies, marmalades and other sweet dishes. But, in many tropical countries, bananas are often prepared as appetizer and main dishes, using salt, pepper, vinegar, garlic, olive oil, onions and other spices. Bananas used for cooking are often called plantains.

Bananas are also used in cosmetology for making nutrient-rich moisturizers and for softening purposes in facial masks and hair.

This book has 44 wonderful figures to make using bananas and everyday fruits such as grapes and blueberries. No need for special skills, just a positive attitude and a sense of humor.

Man

2 bananas

1 small bunch of red grapes

1 blue grape

2 green grapes

1 blueberry

1 One whole banana is the head.

2 Place the small bunch of red grapes on the head. This is the hair. Place two green grapes against the head on either side. These are the ears.

3 Cut a blueberry in half, without fully severing the two halves.

4 Unfold the halves. These are the eyes. Place them on the face.

5 Cut a red grape in half.

6 One half is the nose. Cut the other half in two. These are the lips.

7 Place the lips and nose on the face.

8 Make two vertical incisions from the end to the stem of the second banana.

9 Cut the resulting strip of banana peel in two, without fully severing from the base. These are the hands.

10 Arrange the body next to the head.

11 Use the red grapes for the legs.

12 Cut a blue grape in half lengthwise. These are the boots. Attach the boots to the legs.

Ram

INGREDIENTS

2 bananas
2 red grapes
1 green grape
2 raspberries
blueberries
pomegranate seeds

1 Make two parallel incisions from the end of the banana to the stem, without fully severing the resulting strip of banana peel.

2 Cut this strip of peel in two. These are the horns.

3 Cut one red grape in half lengthwise. These are the ears.

4 Place the ears on the head.

5 Cut the green grape in half without fully severing the two halves. Unfold the halves. These are the eyes.

6 Cut the blueberry in half without fully severing the two halves. Unfold the halves. These are the pupils.

7 Place the pupils on the eyes.

8 Cut the other red grape in half. Cut one half in two. These are the lips.

9 Use two raspberries for the nose. Place the lips and nose on the head.

10 Use one whole banana for the body. Arrange blueberries for the hair.

11 Lay out the pomegranate seeds in the form of legs. Use blue grape halves for the hooves.

Rooster

INGREDIENTS

1 banana
1 red grape
1 green grape
3 raspberries
1 blueberry
6 pomegranate seeds
1 strawberry

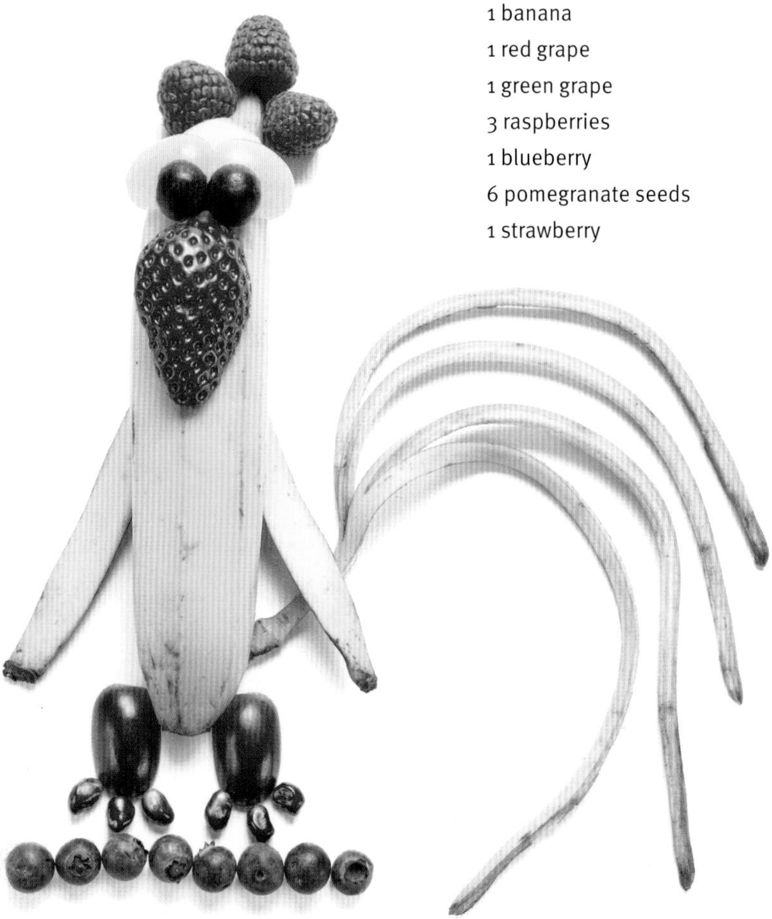

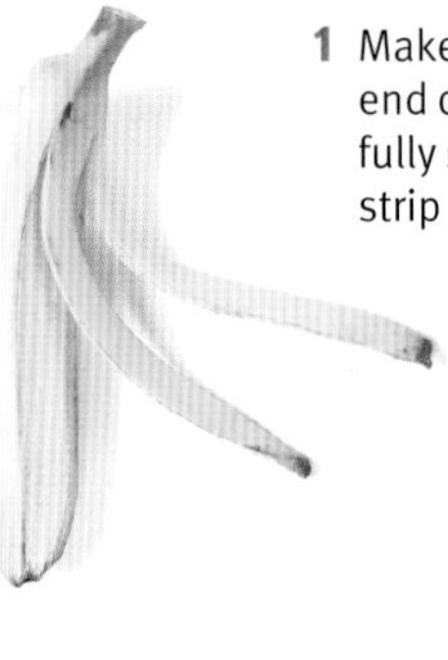

1 Make two parallel incisions from the end of the banana to the stem without fully severing the peel. Cut the resulting strip in two. These are the wings.

2 Lay the banana cut side down. This is the body. Fold the wings under the body.

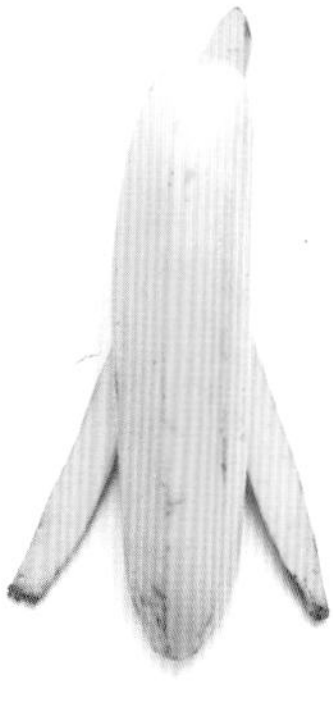

3 Lay out the raspberries in the form of a crest.

4 Cut the green grape in half without fully severing the two halves. Unfold the halves. These are the eyes.

5 Cut the blueberry in half without fully severing the two halves. Unfold the halves. These are the pupils.

6 Place the eyes on the head. Place the pupils on the eyes.

7 Cut a side slice from the strawberry. This is the beak.

8 Place the beak under the eyes.

9 Cut off a strip of peel from a whole banana.

10 Cut this into four small strips. This is the tail. Arrange the tail against the body.

11 Cut the red grape in half lengthwise.

12 These are the legs. Arrange the pomegranate seeds in the form of claws.

Snail

INGREDIENTS

2 bananas
2 red grapes
1 green grape
1 strawberry
1 blueberry

1 Cut off a vertical slice from one side of a banana.

2 Place a wooden skewer against the banana as a guide. This is the preform for the trunk. Make horizontals incisions along the whole preform.

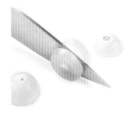

3 Bend the preform in the form of the body.

4 Cut off the tips from the top and bottom of the green grape. Cut the middle part into two rounds, without fully severing the two pieces. Unfold the circles. These are the eyes.

5 Cut off two circular edge pieces from the blueberry. These are the pupils.

6 Place the pupils on the eyes. Place the eyes on the head.

7 Cut two edge pieces from a slice of strawberry.

8 Place them the cut side down. These are the horns. Place them against the head.

9 Cut the second banana into round slices.

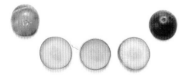

10 Cut the second red grape into round slices.

11 Lay out the snail's shell using the banana slices. Decorate with grape slices.

Poodle

INGREDIENTS
1 banana
1 red grape
1 green grape
1 blue grape
1 strawberry
blueberries

1 Make two parallel incisions from the end of the banana to the stem, without fully severing the peel.

2 Cut the peel strip in two. These are the ears.

3 Place the banana cut side down. This is the head. Attach the ears. Arrange blueberries on the head.

4 Cut the ends off the green grape. Cut the middle piece into two rounds, without fully severing the two pieces. Unfold the rounds. These are the eyes.

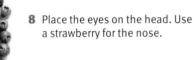

5 Cut off two round edge slices from a blueberry. These are the pupils. Place the pupils on the eyes.

6 Cut the red grape in half lengthwise.

7 Cut one half in two. These are the eyelids.

8 Place the eyes on the head. Use a strawberry for the nose.

9 Lay out the neck, body, legs and tail using the blueberries.

10 Cut the blue grape in half lengthwise. These are the paws.

11 Lay the paws against the legs.

Dragon

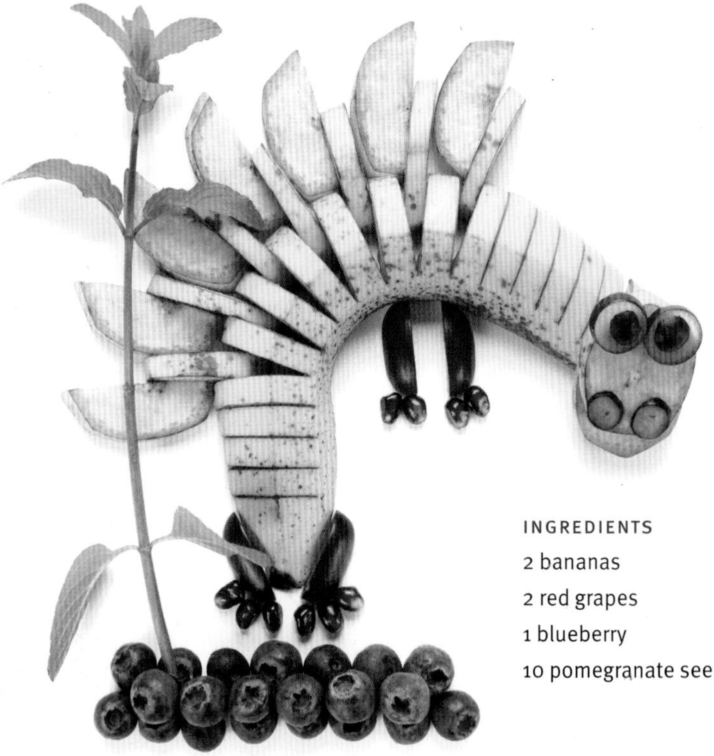

INGREDIENTS

2 bananas
2 red grapes
1 blueberry
10 pomegranate seeds

1 Cut off eight rounds from one banana. One of these is the head. The rest are the spikes.

2 Cut off two round edge slices from a blueberry. These are the pupils. Then cut two rounds. These are the nostrils.

3 Cut off two rounds from the red grape. These are the eyes.

14

4 Place the pupils on the eyes.

5 Place the eyes and nostrils on the head.

6 Cut the banana in half lengthwise as shown. The flat piece without the stem is the preform.

7 Place a wooden skewer against the preform as a guide. Make horizontal incisions along the whole preform.

8 Bend the preform into the form of the body.

9 Cut seven of the banana rounds in half.

10 Insert seven halves into the slots on the body.

11 Put the remaining halves between them. These are the spikes and crest. Lay the banana circle.

12 Lay the last banana round and place the head on top.

13 Cut the red grapes in half. Cut each of the halves into quarters. These are the hands and legs.

14 Place them against the body. Lay out fingers and toes using the pomegranate seeds.

Bull

INGREDIENTS

2 bananas

2 red grapes

1 green grape

2 mint leaves

blueberries

pomegranate seeds

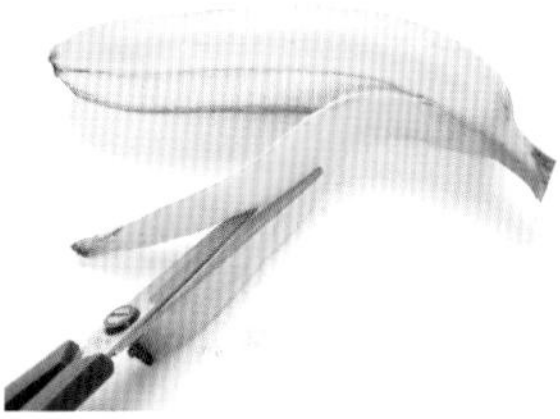

1 Make two parallel incisions from the end of the banana to the stem, without fully severing the peel. Cut the peel strip in two. These are the horns.

2 Place the banana cut side down. This is the head. Bend the horns upwards.

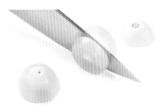

3 Cut off the tips from the green grape. Cut the middle part into two rounds, without fully severing the two pieces. Unfold the rounds. These are the eyes.

4 Cut off two round edge slices from a blueberry. These are the pupils.

5 Place the pupils on the eyes. Use the mint leaves for the ears.

6 Cut off a strip of peel from the second banana. This is the mouth.

7 Cut out teeth as shown. Lay the mouth on the head.

8 Cut a red grape in half without fully severing the two halves. Unfold the halves. This is the nose.

9 Place the nose on the head under the mouth. This is the head.

10 Place a whole banana against the head. This is the body. Use blueberries for the legs and pomegranate seeds for the tail.

11 Cut the second red grape in half, and then cut one half into two parts on an angle. These are the hooves.

12 Place the hooves against the legs.

Grizzly Bear

INGREDIENTS

1 banana
2 red grapes
1 green grape
1 blue grape
1 blueberry
2 pomegranate seeds

1 Cut the end off the banana on an angle as shown. Then cut off five oval slices.

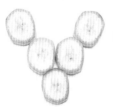

2 Lay out three slices in the form of the head. Place two slices against the head. These are the ears.

3 Cut off one more slice and cut it in half.

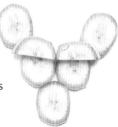

4 Place the halves on the head. These are the forehead.

5 Cut off two edge slices from the green grape. These are the eyelids.

6 Cut the middle part of the grape in half lengthwise without fully severing the two pieces and unfold the halves. These are the eyes.

7 Cut off two round edge slices from the blueberry. These are the pupils.

8 Place the pupils on the eyes.

9 Place the eyes on the head. Add the eyelids. Use two pomegranate seeds for the teeth.

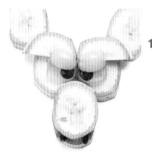

10 Place one banana slice on top. This is the muzzle.

11 Cut a thin slice from the blue grape.

12 Place the blue grape slice cut side down. This is the nose.

13 Use the remaining half of the banana for the body. Lay out four red grape halves for the arms and legs.

Rabbit

2 bananas

1 red grape

4 green grapes

1 blue grape

1 blueberry

1 raspberry

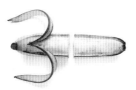

1 Make two parallel incisions from the end of the banana to the stem, without fully severing the peel. Cut the peel strip in two. These are the ears.

2 Cut the banana in half. These are the head and body.

3 Bend the ears upwards.

4 Cut off the tips from a green grape. Cut the middle part into two rounds, without fully severing the two pieces. Unfold the rounds. These are the eyes.

5 Cut off two round edge slices from a blueberry. These are the pupils.

6 Place the pupils on the eyes. Place the eyes on the head.

7 Cut the red grape in half without fully severing.

8 Unfold the halves. These are the cheeks.

9 Cut off half of the blue grape. This is the nose.

10 Place the nose on the cheeks. Use the raspberry for the mouth.

11 Cut two strips of peel from the body, without severing them. These are the arms.

12 Lay the body against the head. Place two grapes against the body. These are the legs.

13 Cut the third grape in half. These are the paws.

21

Cat

INGREDIENTS

1 banana
1 red grape
1 green grape
2 blue grapes

1 Cut the banana in half lengthwise, as shown. The flat piece without the stem is the preform.

2 Place a wooden skewer against the preform as a guide. Make horizontal incisions along the whole preform.

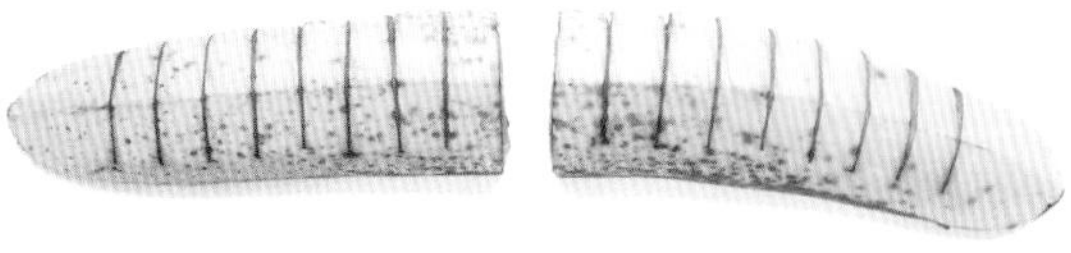

3 Cut the preform in half. These are the head and body.

4 Cut two semicircles from the remaining part of banana. These are the ears. Place them under the head.

5 Cut off a tip from the green grape. Cut the tip in half. These are the eyelids.

6 Cut a round from the remainder of the grape, without fully severing. Cut one more round.

7 Unfold the rounds. These are the eyes.

8 Cut off the tips from a blue grape. Cut one tip in half. These are the pupils.

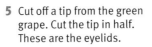

9 Place the eyelids on the eyes. Place the pupils on the eyes under the eyelids. Lay the eyes on the head.

10 Cut the red grape in half without fully severing.

11 Unfold the halves. These are the cheeks. Place them on the muzzle.

12 Cut off half of a blue grape. This is the nose. Place the nose on the cheeks. Lay the body next to the head.

13 Cut three semicircle pieces from the remaining banana. Separate the peel.

14 Make four similar legs and a tail.

Fly

INGREDIENTS

1 banana
1 green grape
1 blue grape
1 strawberry
1 parsley stem

1 Cut four round slices of banana.

2 Make an incision in the peel.

3 Separate the peel symmetrically. Make three similar details.

4 One of these details is the back part of body. Another one is the bottom half of the front part of the body. The strips are the legs.

5 The third detail is the head.

6 Cut a banana round and place it on top of the three details, as shown.

7 Cut a strawberry in half.

8 Cut one half into quarters. These are the wings. Place the wings on the body.

9 Cut the green grape in half. These are the eyes.

10 Place a grape half cut side down. Cut off a slice on an angle. This is the space for the pupil.

11 Cut off a slice on the second grape half for the second pupil.

12 Cut off two rounds from the blue grape. These are the pupils.

13 Place the pupils on the eyes. Place the eyes on the head. Insert a parsley stem between the eyes.

Lion

INGREDIENTS

1 banana

1 blue grape

1 green grape

6 blueberries

3 strawberries

8 pomegranate seeds

1 Cut a whole banana into three parts.

2 Lay the end piece against the middle piece. This is the head.

3 Cut the strawberries into rounds. Lay them out in the form of a mane.

4 Cut off two rounds from the remaining banana third. Place these against the head. These are the ears.

5 Cut off the tips from the green grape. Cut the middle piece in half without fully severing.

6 These are the eyes.

7 Cut off two round edge slices from a blueberry. These are the pupils.

8 Place the pupils on the eyes. Place the eyes on the head.

9 Cut off a thin slice from the blue grape.

10 Place the remaining grape cut side down. This is the nose.

11 Cut a round slice of banana in half.

12 Separate the strips of the peel. One of these strips is the tail.

13 Place the banana part against the head. This is the body. Attach the tail to the body.

14 Lay out the legs using blueberries. Use pomegranate seeds for the toes.

Seahorse

INGREDIENTS

1 banana
1 green grape
1 blueberry
4 raspberries

1 Lay the banana with the stem pointing up. Use a wooden skewer as a guide. Make horizontal incisions until the middle of the banana, without fully severing the peel.

2 Make one more incision nearer to the banana stem, without fully severing it.

3 Fold in the cut part of the top. This is the head. The stem of the banana is the snout.

4 Cut out one wedge segment and arrange slightly off the base. This is the fin.

5 Lay out a crest using the raspberries.

6 Cut off a round slice from the green grape. This is the eye.

7 Cut a blueberry in half. One half is the pupil.

8 Place the pupil on the eye.

9 Place the eye on the head.

Scorpion

INGREDIENTS

1 banana

1 green grape

1 red grape

1 blueberry

1 Cut a banana in half.

2 Cut a slit in the peel down the middle part of the stem half.

3 Make four incisions on each side of the cut.

4 Cut off the peel on the opposite side.

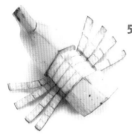

5 Put the half cut side down.
Bend the cut strips of the peel.
These are the legs.

6 Cut a green grape in half
without fully severing.

7 Unfold the halves.
These are the eyes.

8 Cut a blueberry in half
without fully severing.

9 Unfold the halves. These
are the pupils.

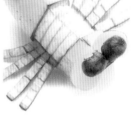

10 Place the pupils on the eyes.
Place the eyes on the head.

11 Lay out the forelegs using
the strips of peel from the
remaining banana half.

12 Cut the red grape in half.
Make incisions in each of
the halves.

13 Press the cut parts
slightly. These are
the claws.

Tiger

INGREDIENTS

1 banana
1 green grape
1 red grape
2 raspberries

1 To make the body and head, lay the banana with the stem pointing up. Using a wooden skewer as a guide, make incisions from the end to the middle of the banana, without fully severing the peel. Make one more incision nearer to the banana stem, without fully severing it.

2 Fold over the stem. Cut out a wedge segment.

3 Separate the peel on each side of the wedge piece. These are the cheeks.

4 Bend the remaining cut piece of banana on the opposite side. This is the body.

5 Insert the blueberries between the first and second incisions. These are the eyes. Use the raspberries for the ears.

6 Attach the cheeks. Cut a red grape in half and place it on top of the cheeks. This is the nose.

7 Cut a red grape in half lengthwise.

8 Cut the green grape in half lengthwise.

9 Cut halves of red and green grapes into semicircles.

10 Lay out the legs from these slices. Make paws from the tip slices.

Mouse

INGREDIENTS

1 banana

1 green grape

1 blue grape

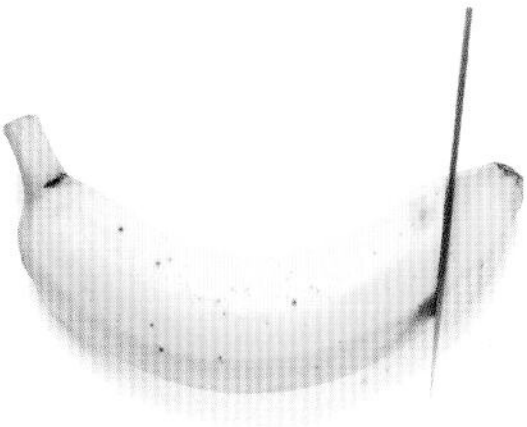

1 Cut off the end of the banana at an angle. This is the head.

2 Cut two round slices from the remainder of the banana and place them under the head. These are the ears.

3 Cut a green grape in half, without fully severing. Unfold the halves. Place them on the head. These are the eyes.

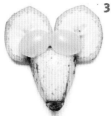

4 Cut off two round tips from the blue grape. These are the pupils.

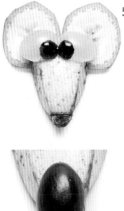

5 Place the pupils on the eyes.

6 Cut a half from the blue grape. This is the nose.

7 Place the nose on the muzzle.

8 Cut a banana slice on an angle.

9 Separate the peel. These are the arms.

10 Cut off a round slice of banana. Cut it into two parts. The smaller part is the leg.

11 Lay out the arms and the leg. Place a round slice of banana on top. This is the body.

12 Make one more leg. Use a strip of banana peel for the tail.

Gnome

1 Cut a banana in half at an angle.

2 Cut a slit in the peel in the middle part of the stem half.

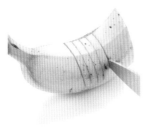

3 Make four incisions on each side of the cut.

4 Cut off the peel on the opposite side of the banana.

5 Put this half cut side down. Bend the cut strips of the peel. These make the hair.

6 Cut off three round slices from a red grape.

7 Two of these are the ears. Place on the head.

8 Cut a green grape in half, without fully severing.

9 Unfold the halves. These are the eyes.

10 Cut the blueberry in half, without fully severing.

11 Unfold the halves. These are the pupils.

12 Place the pupils on the eyes.

13 Place the eyes on the head. Use a raspberry for the nose.

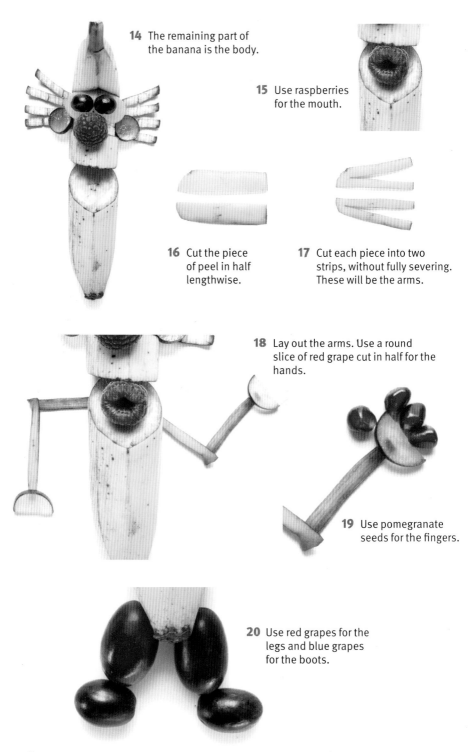

14 The remaining part of the banana is the body.

15 Use raspberries for the mouth.

16 Cut the piece of peel in half lengthwise.

17 Cut each piece into two strips, without fully severing. These will be the arms.

18 Lay out the arms. Use a round slice of red grape cut in half for the hands.

19 Use pomegranate seeds for the fingers.

20 Use red grapes for the legs and blue grapes for the boots.

Pirate

INGREDIENTS

2 bananas
2 green grapes
2 red grapes
3 blue grapes

1. On one banana, cut the banana peel into the narrow strips all the way around.

2. Separate the strips from the banana pulp. This is the hair.

3. Cut off two round edge slices from a green grape.

4. Cut one edge slice in half. These are the eyelids.

5. Cut the middle part of the grape in half, without fully severing. Unfold the halves. These are the eyes.

6. Cut a blue grape in half. One of these is an eye patch.

7. Cut off a segment from the other half. This is a pupil.

8. Place the pupil on one eye. Place the eyelids above and below the pupil of the one eye.

9. Put the eye patch on the other eye. Place the eyes on the head.

10. Cut a red grape in half.

11. Cut out a triangle from one half. This is the nose.

12. Cut another red grape in half. These are the lips.

13 Place the nose and lips on the face.

14 Cut a round slice from the remaining piece of banana. Use the rest for the body.

15 Separate the peel from the round banana slice.

16 Cut it into two strips. These are the arms.

17 Attach two blue grapes to the body. These are the shorts.

18 Cut halves of red and green grapes into semicircles.

19 Lay out the knee socks from them.

20 Cut halves of blue grapes in two. These are the boots.

21 Place the boots against the legs.

Face

INGREDIENTS

1 banana
1 green grape
1 blue grape
raspberries
pomegranate seeds

1 Cut a piece from the end of the banana. This is the nose.

2 Cut off two round slices for the area under the eyes.

3 Cut off the tips from the green grape.

4 Cut one of these in half. These are the eyelids.

5 Cut the middle part of the grape half. These are the eyes.

6 Cut off two round slices from the blue grape. These are the pupils.

7 Place the pupils on the eyes.

8 Place the eyelids on top.

9 Place the complete eyes on the banana rounds. Attach the nose and use two more round slices of banana for the ears.

10 Cut out some peel in the form of a mouth.

11 Cut out teeth as shown. Place the cut peel under the mouth. This is the chin.

12 Use raspberries for the hair.

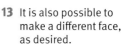

13 It is also possible to make a different face, as desired.

Mermaid

INGREDIENTS

2 bananas
1 green grape
2 red grapes
1 blueberry
2 pomegranate seeds
2 mint leaves

1 Cut the banana peel on one banana into narrow strips all the way around.

2 Separate the strips from the banana pulp. This is the hair.

3 Cut off the tips from the green grape. Cut the middle part of the grape in half. These are the eyes.

4 Cut off two round edge slices from the blueberry. These are the pupils.

5 Place the pupils on the eyes. Place the eyes on the head.

6 Cut a red grape in half.

7 Cut one half in two. These are the eyelids.

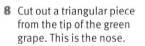

8 Cut out a triangular piece from the tip of the green grape. This is the nose.

9 Place the nose on the face. Use two pomegranate seeds for the lips.

10 Separate the peel from a round slice of banana. These are the arms.

11 Use the second banana for the body. Lay the arms against the body.

12 Cut the red grape in half, without fully severing. Unfold the halves. These are the breasts.

13 Lay out the fin using mint leaves.

Pig

INGREDIENTS

1 banana

1 green grape

1 red grape

1 blueberry

4 pomegranate seeds

1 Cut a banana into two angled pieces.

2 Cut out a wedge in the middle of the smaller part.

3 Join the parts. This is the head. Make a triangular cutting in the peel. This is the ear.

4 Cut out the second ear symmetrically. Bend the ears.

5 The remaining part is the body. Cut out a narrow strip of peel. This is the tail.

6 Twist the tail. Make rectangular incisions for the legs as shown.

7 Cut out the legs from the peel.

8 Insert the legs into the incisions. Attach the body to the head.

9 Cut off the tips from the green grape. Cut the remaining middle part into two round slices, without fully severing. These are the eyes.

10 Place the eyes on the head. Cut off two rounds from the blueberry. These are the pupils. Place on the eyes.

11 Cut the red grape into three slices. Cut one edge slice into two unequal parts.

12 Put the smallest part on the middle slice. This is the mouth.

13 Attach the mouth to the muzzle. Use pomegranate seeds for the hooves.

Prowling Lion

INGREDIENTS

2 bananas

1 blue grape

1 red grape

1 blueberry

1 cherry tomato

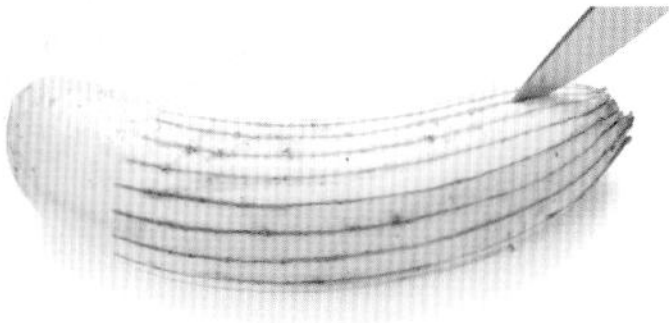

1 Cut the banana peel of one banana into narrow strips all the way around.

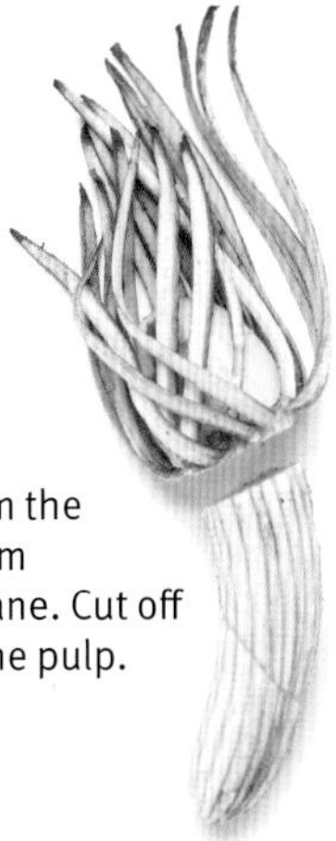

2 Separate the strips from the banana pulp. Bend them upwards. This is the mane. Cut off the remaining part of the pulp.

3 Lay out the mane around the head.

4 Cut the green grape in half, without fully severing. Unfold the halves. These are the eyes.

5 Cut the blueberry in half, without fully severing. Unfold the halves. These are the pupils.

6 Place the pupils on the eyes. Place the eyes on the head.

7 Cut the cherry tomato in half. These are the ears.

8 Attach the ears to the head. Place a round slice of banana below the head.

9 Cut off an edge slice from the red grape. This is the tongue.

10 Place the tongue on the banana round.

11 Place another round of banana on top. This is the muzzle. Place the blue grape on the muzzle. This is the nose.

12 Separate the peel from a banana round. This is the tail.

13 Cut the peel of another two banana rounds into parts. These are the legs.

14 Use the second whole banana for the body. Place the legs and tail under the body.

Hedgehog

INGREDIENTS

1 banana
1 green grape
1 blue grape
1 red grape
1 blueberry

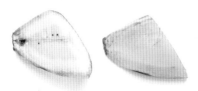

1 Cut off the end of the banana. Cut this in half lengthwise. One half is the head.

2 Cut off eight round slices from the remaining banana. Cut each slice in half.

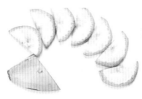

3 Lay out the top line of the needles.

4 Then lay out the first and second lines in overlapping layers.

5 Use the blue grape for the nose.

6 Cut off the tips from the green grape. Cut the middle piece into two rounds, without fully severing. These are the eyes.

7 Cut off two rounds from the blueberry. These are the pupils.

8 Place the pupils on the eyes. Place the eyes on the head.

9 Cut the red grape in half.

10 Cut one half into slices.

11 Take an edge and a middle slice.

12 Place the edge slice on top of the middle one. This is the mouth. Attach the mouth to the muzzle.

13 Separate the peel from semicircle slices of banana. These are the legs.

Frog

INGREDIENTS

1 banana

1 green grape

1 blue grape

1 Cut a banana into three pieces as shown. The large piece is the head. The middle piece is the body.

2 Cut the peel in the form of eyelids.

3 Cut out the mouth.

4 Cut off the lower edge to round off the edges of the head.

5 Cut out the teeth. Open the eyelids.

6 Cut out a narrow segment from the green grape.

7 Cut out a similar segment from the blue grape.

8 Insert the blue segment into the slot in the green grape. This is an eye.

9 Make the second eye. Place the eyes under the eyelids.

10 Cut off four triangular segments from the remaining part of the banana.

11 Separate the peel from these. They are the legs.

12 Bend two of them in the form of hind legs.

13 Attach the body. Arrange the forelegs.

14 Place a round of banana on top of the body.

15 Place the head on top.

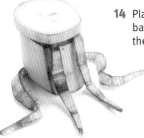

Turtle

INGREDIENTS

1 banana
1 green grape
1 blue grape
3 strawberries

1 Cut off half of the banana at an angle. This is the head.

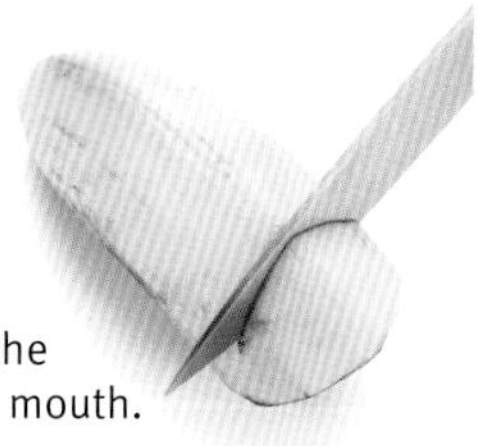

2 Make an incision near the slanted end. This is the mouth.

3 Cut the strawberries into round slices. Lay out them in the form of a shell.

4 Place banana rounds on top.

5 Place three more strawberry slices. Lay one banana slice in the center.

6 Cut off one more round banana slice. Cut it in half. These are the legs.

7 Place the legs next to the shell. Attach the head.

8 Cut the blue grape in half. Cut off a round from one half.

9 Cut the round in half, without fully severing.

10 Unfold the halves. These are the eyes.

11 Cut the green grape in half, without fully severing.

12 Unfold the halves. These are the eyelids.

13 Place the eyelids on the eyes. Place the eyes on the head.

Butterfly

INGREDIENTS

1 banana

1 green grape

1 blue grape

1 red grape

1 strawberry

1 pomegranate seed

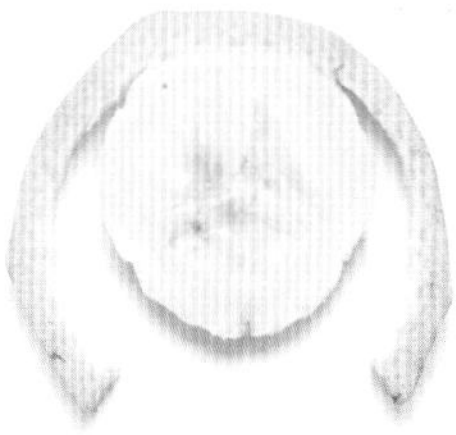

1 Cut off a round slice of banana.

2 Cut the peel. Separate the peel symmetrically.

3 Bend the separated strips of peel upwards. These are the antennae.

4 Cut off half of the green grape.

5 Cut the half into quarters. These are the eyes.

6 Place the eyes on the head.

7 Cut off two round slices from the blue grape. These are the pupils.

8 Place the pupils on the eyes. Use a pomegranate seed for the nose.

9 Cut off a round slice from the red grape. Cut out a segment for the mouth.

10 Place the mouth on the head.

11 Cut off a round slice from the strawberry. Cut the slice in half.

12 Place the strawberry halves standing up below the head. They make the body. Use round slices of banana for the back wings.

13 Cut off two oval slices from the remaining piece of banana.

14 These are the front wings.

Centipede

1 banana

1 green grape

1 blue grape

1 red grape

7 strawberries

2 pomegranate seeds

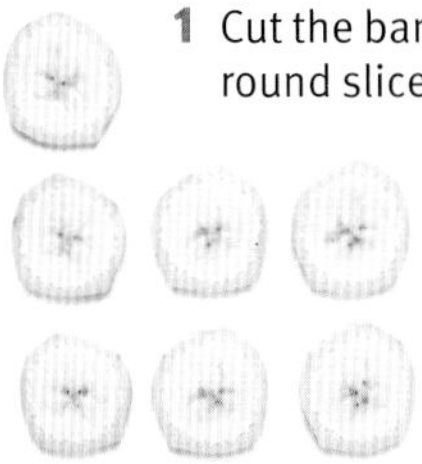

1 Cut the banana into round slices.

2 Cut the peel. Separate the peel symmetrically. Bend the separated strips of peel downwards. These are the legs.

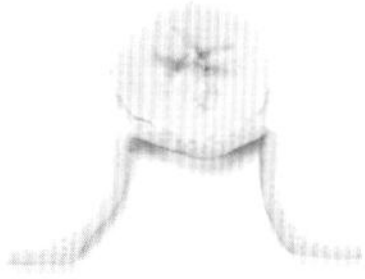

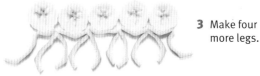

3 Make four more legs.

4 Cut one banana circle in half.

5 Place one half next to the body. This is the neck. Place another half on top. This is the mouth.

6 Cover with round banana slice. This is the head.

7 Cut off half of the green grape. Cut this half into quarters. These are the eyes.

8 Cut off two round slices from the blue grape. These are the pupils.

9 Place the pupils on the eyes. Place the eyes on the head.

10 Cut off a tip from the red grape. This is the nose.

11 Place the nose under the eyes. Use pomegranate seeds for the horns.

12 Cut off the tips from the strawberries.

13 Arrange these in the form of the body.

Young Guy

INGREDIENTS

2 bananas

1 green grape

1 blue grape

1 raspberry

1 pomegranate seed

1 Cut the banana peel of one banana into narrow strips all the way around. Separate the strips from the banana pulp.

2 Bend them upwards. This is the hair. Cut off half of the banana on an angle.

3 This is the head. Use round slices of banana for the ears.

4 Cut off the sides from the green grape.

5 Cut the middle part of the grape in half without severing. Unfold the halves. These are the eyes.

6 Cut one of the side pieces in half. These are the upper and lower eyelids.

7 Cut the blue grape in half. Cut off a semicircle from one half. This is the pupil.

8 Cut off a round slice from the other half. This is the second pupil.

9 Place the pupil on one eye. Attach the eyelids. Place the round pupil on the second eye.

10 Place the eyes on the head. Use the raspberry for the nose. Place a pomegranate seed next to one ear as an earring.

11 Cut out the peel in form of a mouth.

12 Cut out teeth. Attach the mouth to the head.

13 Use an end piece of banana for the body. Make arms and legs from strips of banana peel. Use quarters of the blue grape for the boots.

Crocodile

INGREDIENTS
1 banana
1 green grape
1 blue grape
pomegranate seeds

1 Make two incisions in the peel about one-third from the end of the banana. This will be the tail.

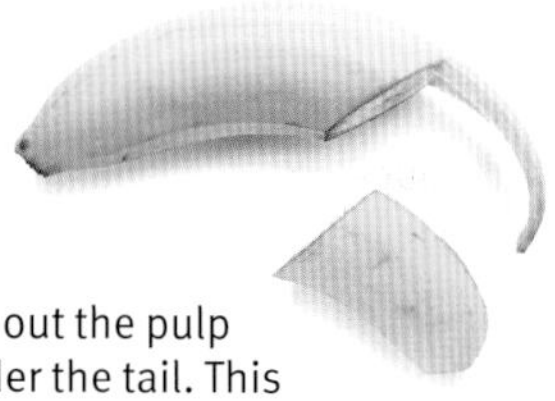

2 Cut out the pulp under the tail. This will be the body.

3 Use a wooden skewer as a guide. Make a cut in the other end of the body without severing the peel. This will be the head.

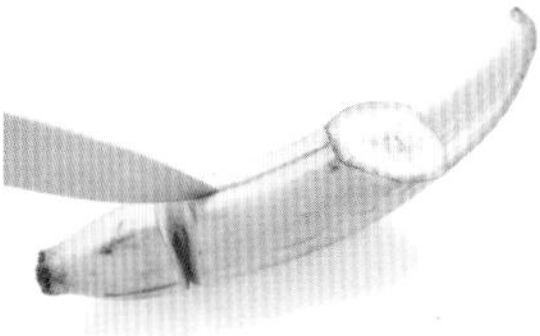

4 Make an incision down the middle of the body.

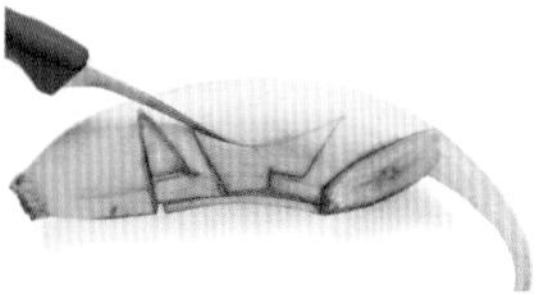

5 Put the body on its side and cut out hind and forelegs as shown.

6 Cut out two symmetrical legs on the opposite side.

7 Turn over the body. Separate the cut legs. Cut out the internal pulp.

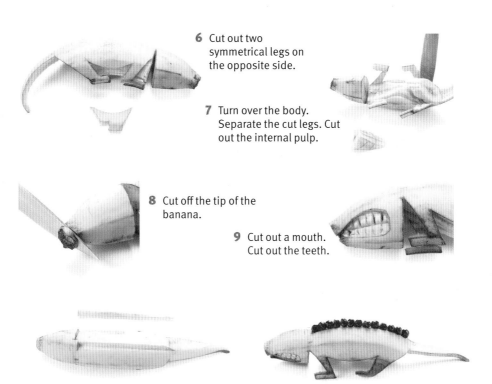

8 Cut off the tip of the banana.

9 Cut out a mouth. Cut out the teeth.

10 Cut out a groove in the center top of the body for fastening a crest.

11 Insert the pomegranate seeds in the groove. This is the crest.

12 Cut a green grape in half, without fully severing. Unfold the halves. These are the eyes.

13 Cut off two rounds from the blue grape. These are the pupils.

14 Place the pupils on the eyes. Place the eyes on the head.

Crab

INGREDIENTS

1 banana
1 green grape
1 red grape
1 blueberry

1 Cut off half of the banana.

2 Cut four strips of peel symmetrically on opposite sides. These are the legs.

3 Separate the strips from the pulp. Cut out the peel between the legs.

4 Cut out the internal pulp.

  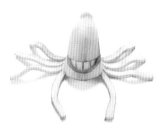

5 Cut out a mouth.

6 Cut out the teeth.

7 Place the crab. Bend the legs.

8 Cut off the tips from the green grape. Cut the middle part of the grape into two rounds without fully severing. Unfold the rounds. These are the eyes.

9 Cut two rounds from the blueberry. These are the pupils.

10 Place the pupils on the eyes. Place the eyes on the muzzle.

11 Cut the red grape in half.

12 Make incisions on each half.

13 These are the claws. Attach the claws to the forelegs.

Horse

INGREDIENTS

2 bananas
1 blue grape
1 red grape
1 blueberry

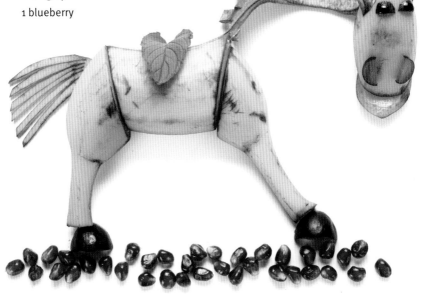

1 Cut off the stem from the banana. This is the leg.

2 Make an angled incision in each end of the banana, as shown, for the head and the body.

3 Draw the contours of the ears.

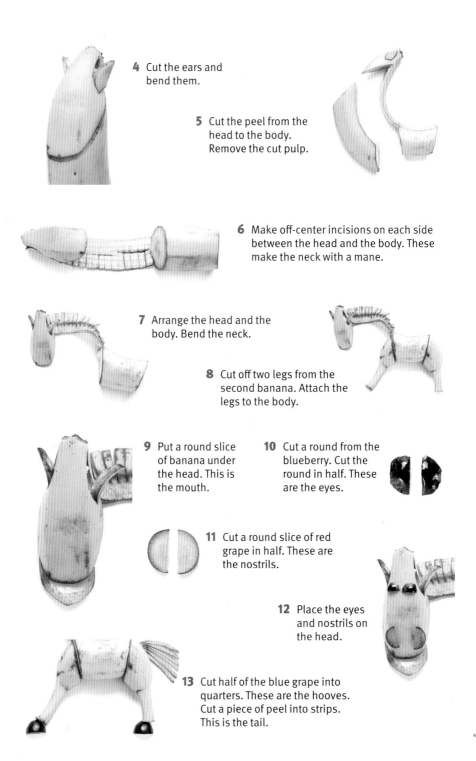

4 Cut the ears and bend them.

5 Cut the peel from the head to the body. Remove the cut pulp.

6 Make off-center incisions on each side between the head and the body. These make the neck with a mane.

7 Arrange the head and the body. Bend the neck.

8 Cut off two legs from the second banana. Attach the legs to the body.

9 Put a round slice of banana under the head. This is the mouth.

10 Cut a round from the blueberry. Cut the round in half. These are the eyes.

11 Cut a round slice of red grape in half. These are the nostrils.

12 Place the eyes and nostrils on the head.

13 Cut half of the blue grape into quarters. These are the hooves. Cut a piece of peel into strips. This is the tail.

Flowers

INGREDIENTS
2 bananas
5 red grapes

1 Cut off the stem from one banana.

2 A short distance from the end of the banana, make a vertical incision halfway into the banana.

3 Make a horizontal cut from the stem end toward the vertical incision. Remove the cut part.

4 Cut five round slices from the second banana.

5 Place the round slices on the open banana.

6 Cut off the tips from the red grapes.

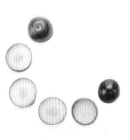

7 Cut the remaining grapes into thin circles.

8 The tips are the middles of the flowers. The circles are petals.

9 Lay out the petals.

10 Place the tips in the center for each flower.

Dog

INGREDIENTS

2 bananas
1 blue grape
1 green grape
1 red grape

1 Cut off the bottom quarter of a banana.

2 Cut out side angles as shown. This is the head.

3 Make an incision for the mouth.

4 Cut off a large piece of banana including the stem. This is the body.

5 Cut out ears from the banana peel.

6 Attach the head to the body. Place the ears under the head.

7 Cut the tip from the blue grape.

8 Cut the tip in half. These are the eyes.

9 Cut off the tip from the green grape. Lay it cut side down and make a center incision, without fully severing.

10 Unfold the halves. These are the eyelids.

11 Place the eyelids on the eyes. Place the eyes on the head.

12 Cut off half of the red grape.

13 This is the nose.

14 Cut legs and a tail from the banana peel.

Ostrich

1 Cut off the end of the banana on an angle.

2 Cut the end in half. These are the hips.

3 Lay out the hips. Cut a further section from the banana. The piece with the stem is the body.

4 Cut off four rounds from the banana.

5 Cut one round in half.

6 Attach one half to the neck. The other half will be used as the base for the beak.

7 Cut a red grape in half lengthwise.

8 Cut out a triangular segment from one half. This is the beak.

9 Place the beak on the base.

10 Cut the remaining half of the red grape in two. Place these next to the beak.

11 Use a round slice of banana for the head. Place the beak on the head.

12 Cut off the tips from the green grape. Cut the middle part in half, without fully severing. Unfold the halves. These are the eyes.

13 Cut off two rounds from a blueberry. These are the pupils.

14 Place the pupils on the eyes. Place the eyes on the head.

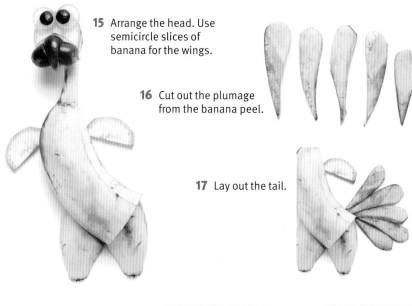

15 Arrange the head. Use semicircle slices of banana for the wings.

16 Cut out the plumage from the banana peel.

17 Lay out the tail.

18 Cut a round of banana in half.

19 Separate the strips of peel. These are the legs.

20 Use pomegranate seeds for the toes.

Clown

INGREDIENTS

1 banana
1 green grape
2 red grapes
2 blue grapes
1 orange cherry tomato
pomegranate seeds

1 Cut off the stem half of the banana. This is the neck and body.

2 Cut the cherry tomato in half. These are the ears.

3 Place the ears on each side of neck.

4 Lay out the pomegranate seeds in form of hair. Place a round slice of banana on top. This is the head.

5 Cut a tip from a blue grape. Cut the tip in half. These are the eyes.

75

6 Cut a tip from the green grape.

7 Put the tip cut side down and make an incision, without fully severing. Unfold the halves. These are the eyelids.

8 Place the eyes under the eyelids.

9 Use around banana slice for the face. Place the eyes on the face. Use half of a red grape for the nose.

10 Lay the face on the head.

11 Cut the other blue grape in half.

12 Put one half cut side down. Cut off part of it for a clown hat.

13 Cut off the middle part from the second half of the blue grape. This is the hat brim.

14 Attach the brim to the hat.

15 Put the hat on the head. Use strips of banana peel for the arms.

16 Cut a red grape in half. These are the hands.

17 Make incisions in each hand. These are the thumbs.

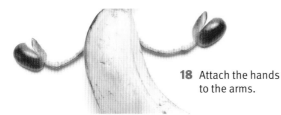

18 Attach the hands to the arms.

19 Cut off the end from the remaining piece of banana.

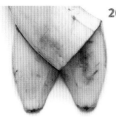

20 Cut this end piece in half lengthwise. Place these under the body. These are the shorts.

21 Cut out legs from banana peel.

22 Use semicircle slices of banana for the boots.

23 It is also possible to make the clown with another pose.

Giraffe

INGREDIENTS

2 bananas

2 green grapes

1 red grape

1 blueberry

pomegranate seeds

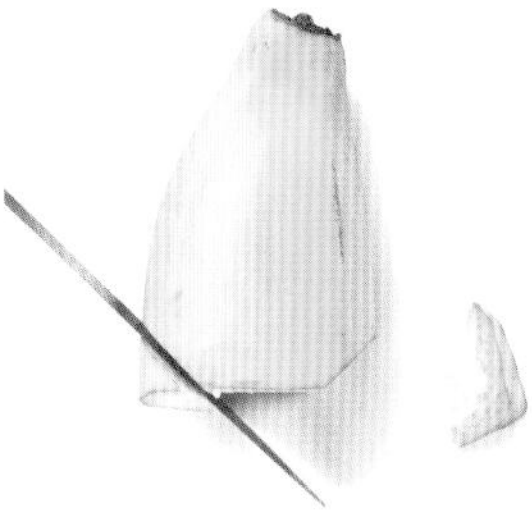

1 Cut off the end of one banana and round off the cut edges. This is the head.

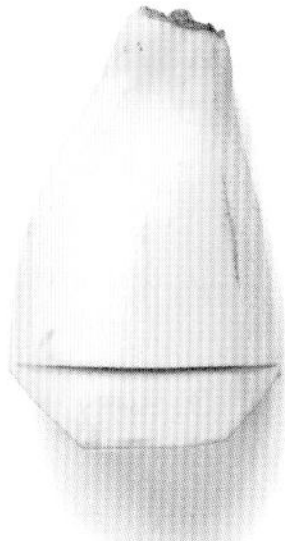

2 Make an incision for the mouth.

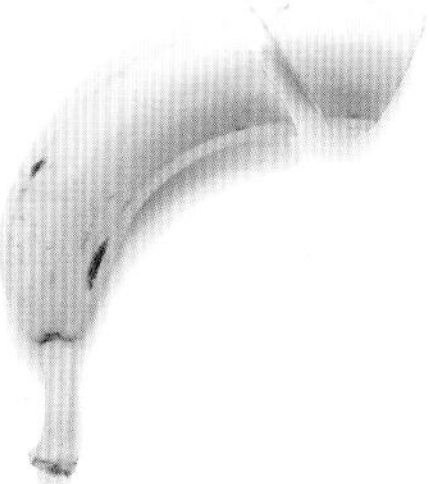

3 Cut off part of the banana for the body.

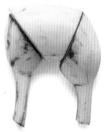

4 Cut off the stem ends of the two bananas for the legs.

5 Cut out the neck from the banana peel.

6 Attach the neck to the body. Place the head on top.

7 Separate the peel from a round slice of banana. Cut it into two strips. One of these is the tail, another one is for the horns.

8 Place the horns under the head. Use two green grape halves for the ears.

9 Cut off the tip from the second green grape. Put it cut side down and make an incision, without fully severing.

10 Unfold the halves. These are the eyelids.

11 Cut the blueberry in half. These are the eyes.

12 Attach the eyelids to the eyes. Place the eyes on the head. Use pomegranate seeds for the nostrils.

13 Cut half of the red grape into quarters. These are the hooves.

14 Attach the hooves and the tail.

Monkey

INGREDIENTS

1 banana
1 green grape
1 red grape
1 blue grape

1 Cut a banana in half.

2 Cut off two round slices from one half. These are the ears.

3 The rest of the banana half is the body. Cut out two strips of peel for an arm and a leg.

4 Cut out one more arm and one more leg symmetrically.

5 Cut out a tail.

6 The second half of the banana is the head. Make an incision for the mouth.

7 Cut off a tip of the blue grape. Cut it in half. These are the eyes.

8 Cut off the tip from the green grape. Place it cut side down and make an incision, without fully severing.

9 Unfold the halves. These are the eyelids. Attach the eyelids to the eyes.

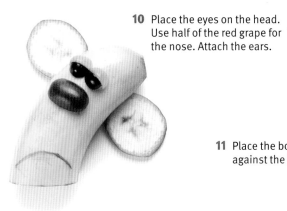

10 Place the eyes on the head. Use half of the red grape for the nose. Attach the ears.

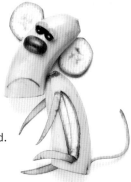

11 Place the body against the head.

Parrot

INGREDIENTS

2 bananas
1 green grape
1 red grape
1 blue grape
mint stem

1 Cut off the end from one banana. Cut off a strip of peel from the remaining piece of banana.

2 Cut the strip in half.

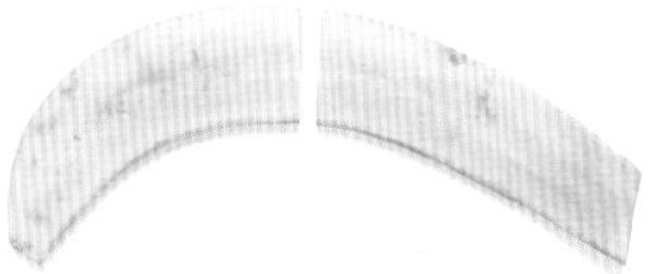

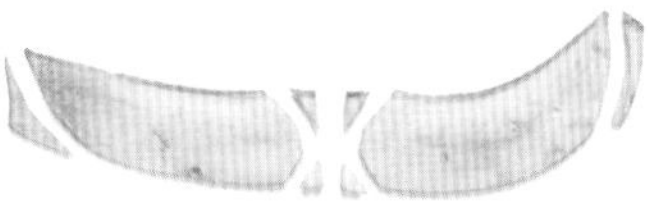

3 Cut out wings as shown.

4 Cut feathers in each of the wings.

5 Cut out one more strip of banana peel.

6 Cut out the tail from it.

7 Lay out the wings and the tail.

8 Cut off half of the second banana on an angle. The stem half is the body.

9 Place the body on the wings and the tail.

10 Make legs and claws from mint stem pieces.

11 Cut off a tip of the blue grape. Cut it in half. These are the eyes.

12 Cut off the tip from the green grape. Place it cut side down and make an incision, without fully severing.

13 Unfold the halves. These are the eyelids. Attach the eyelids to the eyes.

14 Cut out a triangular beak from half of the red grape.

15 Place the eyes and beak on the head.

Bird

INGREDIENTS

2 bananas

1 green grape

1 blueberry

6 pomegranate seeds

2 mint leaves

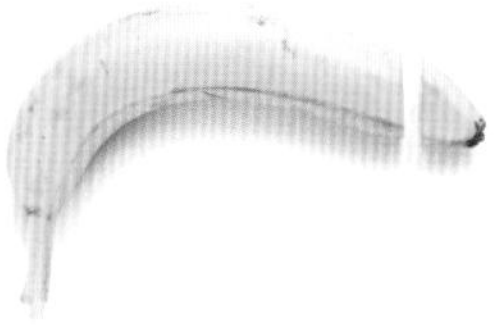

1 Cut off the end of one banana. This is the beak.

2 Cut out triangular segments on each side of beak.

3 Cut out the pulp.

4 Cut off half of the second banana. This is the head and body.

5 Place the beak on the head and mark its shape with a toothpick.

6 Cut out the peel inside the shape and insert the beak.

7 Make holes on the sides of the body for the wings.

8 Use mint leaves for the wings. Insert the wings into the holes.

9 Cut off the tips from the green grape. Cut the middle part into two rounds, without fully severing. Unfold the rounds. These are the eyes.

10 Cut two rounds from a blueberry. These are the pupils.

11 Place the pupils on the eyes. Place the eyes on top of the beak.

12 Make feet from banana peel. Use pomegranate seeds for the toes.

Flower

INGREDIENTS

1 banana
3 green grapes
3 red grapes
1 cherry tomato
5 pomegranate seeds

1 Cut the banana into rounds.

2 Cut three rounds in half.

3 Place five halves cut side down in the form of a star.

4 Place five rounds between the halves. These are petals.

5 Cut the green grapes in half lengthwise.

6 Lay the grape halves on the petals.

7 Put the cherry tomato in the center of the flower. Decorate with pomegranate seeds.

8 Cut a banana round in half.

9 Separate the peel from one half. This is the stem.

10 Place the other half against the stem. This is the leaf.

11 Cut the red grapes in half lengthwise.

12 Cut each half into quarters.

13 Lay out the quarters in the form of a vase.

Palm Tree and Monkey

INGREDIENTS

1 banana

1 blue grape

3 green grapes

8 raspberries

1 Cut the end off the banana on an angle.

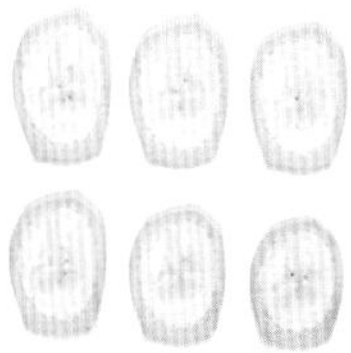

2 Cut off six oval slices.

3 Cut each slice in half lengthwise. These are palm branches.

4 Lay out the stem. Attach two branches.

5 Then lay out the remaining branches.

6 Cut a green grape in half lengthwise.

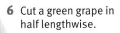

7 Cut off a segment from one end for the eyes. This is the head.

8 Cut off a narrow segment from the opposite side. The muzzle will sit here.

9 Cut out a wedge segment from the blue grape.

10 Cut the tips off the wedge. Cut the middle piece in two. These are the eyes.

11 The other half of the green grape is the muzzle. Cut out a segment for the mouth.

12 Cut two rounds from another green grape. These are the ears.

13 Place the head on the ears. Place the muzzle on the head.

14 Use a slice of banana for the body. Use strips of peel for the arms, legs and tail.

Aster

INGREDIENTS
1 banana
1 stem of mint
pomegranate seeds

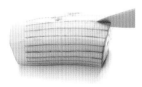

1 Cut the banana in half.

2 Cut off the end.

3 Cut the peel into thin strips all the way around the banana.

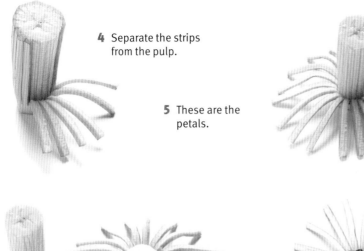

4 Separate the strips from the pulp.

5 These are the petals.

6 Cut out the superfluous pulp.

7 Place pomegranate seeds on the cut.

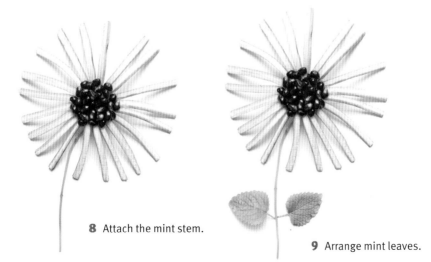

8 Attach the mint stem.

9 Arrange mint leaves.

Rat

INGREDIENTS

1 banana
1 green grape
1 red grape
1 blueberry

1 Cut a banana in half. The stem half is the head.

2 Cut out an ear from the peel.

3 Cut out the second ear symmetrically.

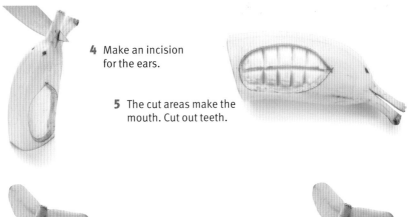

4 Make an incision for the ears.

5 The cut areas make the mouth. Cut out teeth.

6 Insert the ears.

7 Use the second half of the banana for the body.

8 Cut off two rounds from the green grape. These are the eyes. Cut two rounds from the blueberry. These are the pupils.

9 Place the pupils on the eyes.

10 Place the eyes on the head.

11 Cut out a tail from banana peel.

12 Attach the tail. Use a red grape for the nose.

Octopus

INGREDIENTS

1 banana

1 green grape

1 blueberry

1 raspberry

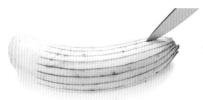

1 Cut the banana peel into narrow strips all the way around.

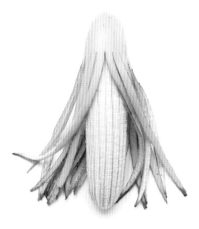

2 Separate the strips from the banana pulp. These are the tentacles.

3 Bend them upwards.

4 Cut the green grape in half, without fully severing.

5 Unfold the halves. These are the eyes.

6 Cut the blueberry in half, without fully severing.

7 Unfold the halves. These are the pupils.

8 Place the pupils on the eyes.

9 Place the eyes on the head. Use a raspberry for the mouth.

A FIREFLY BOOK

Published by Firefly Books Ltd. 2017

Copyright © 2017 Good Mood Editions Gmbh
Text copyright © 2017 Iryna Stepanova, Sergiy Kabachenko
Images copyright© 2017 Iryna Stepanova, Sergiy Kabachenko

First printing

PUBLISHER CATALOGING-IN-PUBLICATION DATA (U.S.)
A CIP record for this title is available from Library of Congress

LIBRARY AND ARCHIVES CANADA CATALOGUING IN PUBLICATION
A CIP record for this title is available from Library and Archives Canada

Published in the United States by
Firefly Books (U.S.) Inc.
P.O. Box 1338, Ellicott Station
Buffalo, New York 14205

Published in Canada by
Firefly Books Ltd.
50 Staples Avenue, Unit 1
Richmond Hill, Ontario L4B 0A7

Cover and interior design: Peter Ross / Counterpunch Inc.

Printed in China

Canada [+] We acknowledge the financial support of the Government of Canada.

MIX
Paper from
responsible sources
FSC
www.fsc.org **FSC® C016973**